Jewish Ceremonial Art

Jewish Ceremonial Art

by

Joseph Gutmann

South Brunswick
New York • Thomas Yoseloff • London

© 1964 By A. S. Barnes and Company, Inc.
Library of Congress Catalogue Card Number: 64-12891

Thomas Yoseloff, Publisher
Cranbury, New Jersey

Thomas Yoseloff Ltd
18 Charing Cross Road
London W.C. 2, England

First Printing November, 1964
Second Printing January, 1968

6065
Printed in the United States of America

Preface

THE STUDY OF THE CEREMONIAL ART OF THE JEWS IS STILL IN ITS INFANCY. RARELY MENTIONED in books devoted to art history, seldom seen in exhibitions of silver, Jewish ceremonial objects are scattered in public and private collections in America, Europe, and Israel. No systematic photographic archives exists of the numerous and diverse objects that are extant; many priceless treasures, never photographed, were destroyed in the Nazi holocaust; few scientific studies on the origin and development of the ceremonial objects of the Jews have appeared to date. Of necessity, therefore, any essay dealing with the ceremonial art that has graced the life of the Jews may hope only to stimulate interest in a much-neglected field of study, rather than endeavor to summarize the results of previous research efforts.

Within the limited scope of this book, no attempt is made to discuss, or even to list, all of the ceremonial objects used by Jews; instead, emphasis is placed on choosing objects which have aesthetic appeal, and which are used in the most representative Jewish ceremonies. I do not offer this explanation by way of apology, but rather in the ardent hope that my small contribution will arouse greater interest in what is, for all practical purposes, a new field of study. I hope, in short, that this work will soon be superseded by a more thorough-going analysis of the nature and scope of the ceremonial art of the Jews.

It is with considerable pleasure that I take this opportunity to thank Dr. Heinrich Feuchtwanger, of the Bezalel National Museum, Jerusalem, Israel for suggesting that I write this work and for his generous help in carefully reading the manuscript. Sincere thanks are also due my colleagues, Professors Stanley F. Chyet, Robert L. Katz, Eugene Mihaly, Jakob J. Petuchowski, and Werner Weinberg, all of the Hebrew Union College–Jewish Institute of Religion, Cincinnati, Ohio, for reading the manuscript and offering valuable suggestions. I wish to record my debt to Professor Guido Schoenberger of New York, for his assistance, and to Professor Emeritus Franz Landsberger of the Hebrew Union College–Jewish Institute of Religion, both for his gracious help and for his genuine interest in my work. My greatest debt on the scholarly side is owed to my teacher, friend, and colleague, Professor Ellis Rivkin, of the Hebrew Union College–Jewish Institute of Religion, for his unfailing interest and his penetrating criticisms. Above all, I wish to acknowledge the generous assistance of my wife Marilyn, whose part in the preparation of this volume amounts virtually to collaboration. To her, I affectionately dedicate this book.

JOSEPH GUTMANN

Contents

Jewish Ceremonial Art

Introduction

ALTHOUGH THE EARLIEST EXTANT CEREMONIAL OBJECTS OF THE JEWS DATE FROM THE MIDDLE Ages, the high regard in which the Jews held fashioners of religious art is manifest at the very dawn of Israel's recorded history, when we read that Bezalel was filled with "the spirit of God, with wisdom, intelligence, and knowledge in every craft: to devise artistic designs, to work in gold, silver, and copper, to cut stones for setting and to carve wood—to work in every craft" (Exod. 31:3–5). Nowhere in ancient annals is the artist-craftsman endowed by his god with talents as diverse as those ascribed to Bezalel, or presented as so intimately involved with the ultra-sacred function of furnishing a sanctuary for his god. Even more noteworthy, however, is the fact that the ancient Hebrews, possessing neither the artistic skills nor heritage of their more sophisticated and cultured neighbors in Egypt and Mesopotamia, felt the need to create and to retroject into their sacred history a lofty artistic tradition as well as a legendary artistic genius like Bezalel, who stands unparalleled in surviving ancient texts.[1]

Prior to the Hellenistic period, the artist—craftsmen of the kingdoms of Judah and Israel produced sacred cult objects for the official centralized sanctuary or Temple established in each of the two monarchies. They may also have fashioned cult objects for the various sacred shrines that, at times, flourished in these kingdoms without official sanction.

New opportunities for the craftsman's skills probably came during the Hellenistic period with the rise of the Pharisaic movement and the introduction of decentralized houses of prayer—synagogues.[2] In addition, the gradually developing ceremonial practices in the home and synagogue probably inspired artistic activity. Unfortunately, however, little evidence of ceremonial objects has survived from this early period.

Even from the medieval period, there is a great paucity of extant objects, a fact quite understandable in view of the medieval practice of melting down objects made of precious metals in order to mint coins or fashion new objects. Also, most of the ceremonial objects that had been created were undoubtedly lost, destroyed or stolen, due to the continuous forced migrations suffered by the Jews in many communities.

Hence, the history of the surviving ceremonial art of the Jews must be viewed within the context of the Jewish involvement in the Christian and Islamic civilizations. What

[1] Joseph Gutmann, "The 'Second Commandment' and the Image in Judaism," *Hebrew Union College Annual*, XXXII (1961), pp. 161-174.
[2] Ellis Rivkin, "Ben Sira and the Nonexistence of the Synagogue: A Study in Historical Method," *In the Time of Harvest: Essays in Honor of Abba Hillel Silver on the occasion of his 70th Birthday*, ed. by Daniel J. Silver. New York and London, 1963, pp. 320-54.

emerges from a study of the role of the Jews as patrons and fashioners of ceremonial art is not a uniform picture, but rather an intricate and involved pattern which varies from civilization to civilization, from country to country, and from century to century.

In many parts of the Islamic world—Yemen and North Africa, for example—the Jews enjoyed a virtual monopoly of the metal trade, for smithery was one of the occupations considered unworthy of a Muslim. Though most of the works produced in these areas are anonymous, we can be relatively certain that most of the Jewish ceremonial objects fashioned there were made by Jewish craftsmen.

In many countries of the medieval Christian world, by contrast, Jewish participation in the crafts was virtually eliminated by the restrictive nature of Christian craft guilds. In Southern France, however, and in Spain and Sicily, where the Islamic influence never totally disappeared, Jews did play a significant role in the crafts, often had their own craft guilds, and probably fashioned their own ceremonial objects. We know that in 1147 the Norman King Roger II brought captive Jewish silk weavers from the Peloponnesian and Ionian Isles to Sicily, where he employed them in his workshops at Palermo. Jewish carpenters too assumed importance in Sicily. One fifteenth-century master carpenter, Joseph Caschisi, distinguished himself in the construction of the royal palace and was appointed warden of the Jewish carpenters' guild of Palermo. In fact, the role of the Jewish craftsman in Sicily was so vital that, when the expulsion of all Jews was ordered by Ferdinand of Spain at the end of the fifteenth century, some of the high Christian officials in Sicily demanded a postponement; they undoubtedly feared that the sudden removal of the Jews would raise prices considerably, because of the lack of Christian craftsmen. The contemporary Jewish traveler, Obadiah of Bertinoro, visiting Palermo in 1487/1488, recorded his amazement at the rich religious appurtenances of the synagogue. He was particularly impressed by the many Torah scrolls "with their cases, surmounted by crowns, and their *rimmonim* (headpieces) of silver and precious stones at the ends of the staves." Of the ceremonial objects produced in Sicily, however, few examples of what may have been Jewish workmanship have survived—the earliest known Torah headpieces, now in the Cathedral Treasury of Palma (Mallorca), are said to have come from the fifteenth-century Sicilian Jewish community of Camarata (Fig. 1).

The Jewish craftsmen in Spain played no less a role than those in Sicily. Indeed, they were so active and so numerous in most of the crafts that several streets in the Jewish quarter of Saragossa were named after the type of craftsmen who resided there.

During Spain's economic prosperity in the thirteenth and fourteenth centuries, the Jews worked not only on behalf of their fellow Jews, but for Christians as well. The disruption that beset Spanish society in the fifteenth century, however, led to restrictive measures against the Jews; in 1415, for example, a bull of Pope Benedict XIII clearly decreed that Jews in Spain were not to be allowed to "fashion or repair a cross, chalice, or sacred vessels."

Although there are no extant examples of the Jewish ceremonial objects wrought in Spain during these centuries, a clue to the magnificence of the works produced by Jewish goldsmiths can be gleaned from depictions of ceremonial objects in surviving fourteenth-century Spanish illuminated Hebrew manuscripts.

In Western Europe, particularly in Germany, the Christian guilds exercised such complete control that, with few exceptions, they managed to keep the Jews from competing with them in the crafts until the eighteenth century, a time when guilds were losing their monopolistic control over the production of goods. Despite these restrictive practices, however, several Jewish craftsmen, who worked in crafts not directly under guild control, were able to obtain special permission to perfect their skills. A Jewish craftsman in Germany, Meir Jaffe, was so highly skilled in the art of leather tooling that the Nürnberg Council asked him to bind a Pentateuch in 1468.

With the exclusion of Jews from the Christian guilds, the need for Jewish ceremonial objects was filled, especially in Germany, by the foremost Christian artists. Thus many ceremonial objects used by the Jews of the seventeenth and eighteenth centuries bear the makers' marks of such well known silversmiths as Johann Conrad Weiss, of Nürnberg, Markus or Matthäus Wolff, of Augsburg, and Jeremias Zobel, of Frankfurt am Main (Fig. 3). These objects, which are among the finest in existence today, were often commissioned by the Court Jews—a small group of Jews who functioned as provisioners of the princely armies in the many territorial states of Germany and as suppliers of luxury goods to the nobles. Affluent and privileged, the Court Jews were in a position to have precious ceremonial objects fashioned for their private home use or for donation to their synagogues. Whereas silver objects in Germany were usually commissioned from Christian craftsmen, elaborately embroidered curtains for the synagogue were specifically made by Jews. Some magnificent examples have survived of the handiwork of two eighteenth-century South German Jewish embroiderers, Elkanah Naumburg of Fürth, and Jakob Koppel Gans, of Hochstadt (Figs. 20, 21).

In Eastern Europe, especially in Poland, Bohemia, and Moravia, Jews were active in the crafts from medieval times. Sixteenth-century Prague had Jewish master-craftsmen, who were granted special royal permission to cater to both Jewish and non-Jewish clients. The competition of these Jewish craftsmen was bitterly resented by the Christian artisan guilds, especially since the high prices set by the guilds caused the poorer classes to turn to the less expensively priced goods of the Jewish artisans.

Since the laws of the Christian artisan guilds forbade the Jews to affix a maker's mark on their objects, it is extremely difficult to determine whether many of the pieces which have survived were produced by Jewish craftsmen. In some cases, however, we can be certain that objects were created by Jewish artisans; the Jewish cemetery in Prague, for instance, contains many tombstones inscribed with the designation "goldsmith" (zoref in Hebrew, or zlatnik in Czech). In 1753, one Jewish artisan, Joshua Zlatnik, even signed his name to a Torah shield, which is now housed in Prague's Jewish Museum.

Within Bohemia and Moravia the art of embroidery also flourished. Some of the magnificent curtains for the Torah ark, among the oldest and finest in existence today—now also in the Jewish Museum at Prague—are mainly the work of Jewish embroiderers.

In Poland, especially in the towns and cities owned by the nobility, Jews engaged in the crafts on a major scale from the seventeenth century on. Here they were given a free hand to become craftsmen, since the great nobles of the privately owned towns and cities needed Jews to compete with craftsmen in the royal towns and cities.

To be sure, in a few cities such as Grodno, in 1652, the Jews were accepted into a number of Christian guilds, from which, though waiving social and religious benefits, they derived professional advantages. Jewish artisans of unique talent were at times also employed by the city guilds. In one instance, in Warsaw at the end of the eighteenth century, when the Jews were being expelled from that city, the city guilds requested that three Jewish silversmiths and five seal engravers be allowed to remain, as they were the only ones possessing these needed skills. Generally, however, although they appealed to local authorities and to the crown, the Jews were denied admission to Christian guilds. Thus, in seventeenth-century Eastern Europe, Jews began to organize their own guilds (*chevrot* in Hebrew), which were patterned after their Christian counterparts and stringently regulated the professional work of their members.

While in the Catholic countries of Eastern Europe the Jews assumed a vital role as artisans, the situation was different in the Protestant middle-class states of seventeenth- and eighteenth-century Holland and England. There the Jews—and particularly the wealthy descendants of former Iberian Jews who had been baptized as Catholics and had later reverted to Judaism—played no important role in the crafts. Instead, the authorities encouraged them to engage in international trade and commerce in order to further mercantile capitalism. Some of the affluent Jews ordered elegant ceremonial objects, such as eighteenth-century silver lamps and Torah headpieces, from such well-known Christian masters as Hermanus van Gulik (Fig. 39) and Otto Knoop in Holland, and from John Ruslen, Gabriel Sleath, and William Grundy in England. Yet some Jews were craftsmen, too. Several works have survived of a London Jewish silversmith, Abraham de Oliveyra (d. 1750), who was frequently commissioned by Jewish congregations and whose goldsmith mark was entered at Goldsmiths Hall in London (Figs. 4, 27).

After the French Revolution, France legally banned the monopolistic control that the guilds had exercised over the crafts, and by the end of the nineteenth century most European countries had followed suit, granting Jews the freedom to enter any craft.

In the United States, the Constitution guaranteed the Jews political, juridical, and economic equality with non-Jews. Even prior to its adoption, there were no monopolistic guilds, hereditary aristocracy, or privileged church to abrogate these rights, and the Jews, therefore, had unrestricted opportunity to obtain training as craftsmen and to serve a market that was both Jewish and non-Jewish. Consequently, it is not surprising to find that one of the most noted silversmiths of early America was a Jew, Myer Myers (1723–1795). His distinction and reputation were such that in 1786 he was elected chairman of the New York Gold and Silversmith Society. Among the works he produced were silver objects for the churches of the wealthy mercantile families, as well as Torah headpieces for the Jewish congregations of Philadelphia, Newport, and New York (Figs. 5a, b).

Since World War II, a new and exciting chapter in ceremonial art has begun, particularly in the United States. Under the inspiration of such enterprising and outstanding architects as the late Eric Mendelsohn and Percival Goodman, many new synagogues have integrated contemporary ceremonial art, produced by Jewish and non-Jewish artists, with modern architectural design, and have thus created an over-all harmonious synthesis. The artists who fashion the religious art for these synagogues employ traditional Jewish religious symbols, but endeavor to express them in modern forms. Through this new aesthetic awareness in modern synagogues, art is allowed to play a prominent role and at the same time to deepen the Jewish religious experience.

Ceremonial Art for the Synagogue

"THIS IS MY GOD AND I WILL BEAUTIFY [LITERALLY: GLORIFY] HIM." IT IS THUS THAT RABBINIC tradition renders the verse in Exod. 15:2. Such an interpretation imposes upon the Jew the requirement that all the objects he uses in the performance of his religious duties be aesthetically pleasing, so that he may worship God in the "beauty of holiness."

Here we perceive a difference in the way most appurtenances are used in Jewish and in Catholic worship. In Catholic worship artistic appurtenances are primarily an integral part of the ritual drama that serves to invoke the redeeming power of the actual Divine presence; in Judaism, however, their predominant function is to enhance religious worship of the Invisible Deity. Thus, in Judaism these objects are used ceremonially as a means to approach the Godly, and they exert an influence only on the worshiper, while in Catholicism they affect God, through the sacraments, and are the means whereby the Divine becomes manifest within the ritual cultic drama.

The ceremonial objects of the Jews revolve around religious worship in the synagogue and the home, the holidays, and the observances of the life cycle. Their history and their forms are as diverse as is Judaism itself. Sometimes ceremonial objects were introduced by the decree of religious leaders; at other times, adapted from the dominant cultural environment in which the Jews lived, they only gradually assumed religious significance. Sometimes they were rejected by religious leaders and came to lose their significance; at other times, under the impact of new cultural conditions, old ceremonies and the objects associated with them were reinterpreted and flourished anew.

The center of Jewish worship focuses on the Torah, or pentateuchal scroll, which is generally housed in a specially built and often elaborately decorated ark, placed inside the synagogue on its eastern wall. The Torah is handwritten on parchment by specially trained scribes; its text is entirely without illustration or decoration. Unlike most ancient scrolls, which roll from end to end around a single stave, the Torah scroll is rolled towards its center, utilizing two staves instead of one.

These staves, each one known as an *ez chayyim,* a "tree of life"—a term also applied to the entire Torah—are adorned with precious metal ornaments now generally called *rimmonim* (literally: pomegranates). During the early medieval period, these Torah ornaments were, in all likelihood, not removable but a part of the staves themselves, as is indicated in fourteenth-century illuminated Hebrew manuscripts that depict synagogue interiors. In

15

the course of time, however, these ornaments became removable and even more elaborate. The headpieces produced in Europe generally abandoned the shape of the fruits they may originally have had and commonly assumed an architectural tower shape. The earliest surviving *rimmonim,* from fifteenth-century Sicily, are fashioned in the shape of square towers with pointed turrets and adorned with typical Moorish horseshoe arches (Fig. 1). In Western Europe, the architectural tower shape became the preferred form of *rimmonim,* with an infinite number of variations on the same theme.

In seventeenth- and eighteenth-century Italy, *rimmonim* were often constructed in the form of a three-tiered steeple with scrolled buttresses or bouquets of flowers which terminated in a flower-filled vase. Extending below the actual headpieces were long chains with bells on them (Fig. 2).

In Frankfurt am Main, in the early eighteenth century, a popular form was the hexagonal turret of three stories, surmounted by an open-work crown and a ball finial (Fig. 3).

Dutch *rimmonim,* with their baroque turret form, exerted an influence on early eighteenth-century English pieces. In England, the turret form was subsequently changed into three bulbous sections of diminishing size, often pierced with foliage and floral patterns, the whole surmounted by a crown finial, as in the beautiful pair made by Abraham de Oliveyra in 1724 (Fig. 4).

A slight variation of the English models was fashioned by Myer Myers in colonial America around 1770. Instead of having the bulbous sections appear in order of diminishing size, Myers' delicate *rimmonim* emphasize the middle section by making it the largest (Figs. 5a, b).

Jewish tradition likened the Torah not only to a tree of life, but to a bride and the daughter of a king; like a bride or a princess, it was to be regally adorned. Among the regal adornments developed in the Middle Ages, along with the *rimmonim,* was the crown (*atarah,* later called *keter torah*), which was placed on top of the Torah staves. These crowns, at first used for special holidays only, were usually placed by themselves on the Torah staves in Germany and Eastern Europe, whereas in Italian synagogues the crown and the *rimmonim* were often used together. Information regarding the shapes of the medieval crowns is scant. From a contract of 1439, we learn of a Torah crown that a Christian goldsmith agreed to fashion for the Jewish community of Arles. It was to be hexagonal and to resemble a medieval city wall with towers at each corner.

Most of the surviving crowns are from the eighteenth century. In Italy, these were usually cylindrical and richly ornamented with shell forms, fruits, blossoms, and scrolled cartouches enclosing such traditional symbols as the *menorah* (candelabrum) and the Tablets of the Law (Plate I). In Germany they were sometimes modeled after royal crowns (Fig. 6).

The most elaborate Torah crowns come from Eastern Europe, especially from Poland. Here lions, griffins, and stags were used to support some of the double- and even tripletiered constructions. The tiers themselves were richly and whimsically decorated with flowers, fruits, animals, zodiacal signs, and semi-precious stones (Fig. 7).

Modern Torah crowns often employ traditional forms, but in accordance with current taste, generally tend to discard superfluous ornamentation in order to allow the material itself to express its intrinsic beauty (Fig. 8).

In most Muslim communities, the Torah scroll was enclosed in a cylindrical or octagonal case (*tik* or *nartik*) made of wood or metal. These cases consisted of two equal parts held together with a hinge at the back. The staves of the Torah often protruded from the case and had headpieces placed on them, which at times assumed the shape of pomegranates (Fig. 9). When the Torah was to be read, the case was opened and the Torah placed upright on the reading desk—unlike the practice in most Western communities, where the Torah, covered with a textile mantle when not in use, is read lying flat on a reading desk.

An interesting modern adaptation of the oriental Torah case was fashioned by Ludwig Wolpert, one of the pioneers of contemporary ceremonial art, and given to a former President of the United States, Harry S. Truman, on behalf of the State of Israel. Wrought of copper and silver, the cylindrical case and the crown surmounting it are decorated with Hebrew lettering (Fig. 10).

In most European communities, the Torah scroll was dressed in beautiful textiles. This practice dates back to early times, for we read in the Talmud that the Torah scroll is to be wrapped "with beautiful silks" (*Shabbat* 133b). One type of textile adornment was the binder (*mappah*) which was tightly wound around the scroll. In Italy, such binders were usually embroidered on precious silk fabrics by women. They carried the name of the donor, or sometimes the occasion—a wedding, for instance—in honor of which they had been given to the synagogue. It was customary, particularly in Southern Germany from the late Middle Ages on, to cut into three or four pieces the linen cloth upon which a boy was circumcised, to stitch the pieces together, and to make from them a Torah binder (called *Wimpel*). The *Wimpel* were usually presented to the synagogue on the occasion of the child's first visit there. Embroidered on the *Wimpel* at first, and painted on in later times, was the name of the boy, the date of his birth, and the standard formula: "May the Lord raise him up to the study of Torah, to the nuptial canopy, and to good deeds." Many symbols were embroidered, or painted, above the inscriptions; after the word for "nuptial canopy" (*chuppah*), for example, an actual marriage ceremony was often depicted (Plate II). Charming expressions of folk art, these binders are also an important source of historical information. Several examples of *Wimpel* dating from 1570 were housed in the synagogue of Worms before they, along with the entire structure, were destroyed by the Nazis.

The Torah scroll was clothed in addition with a mantle (*me'il*) made of such textiles as silk, velvet and brocade. In Ashkenazic (German–Polish) congregations, the mantles generally had stiff tops and were open only at the bottom. They often bore inscriptions, traditional symbols and semi-precious stones. In most Sephardic (Spanish–Portuguese) congregations, the mantles usually had a soft top with an opening at the back. Their beauty lies primarily in the precious textiles and the rich embroideries that were used. Some magnificent mantles of this latter type have survived from eighteenth-century Holland and Italy. In Holland they feature orphreys of velvet embroidered with gold and silver thread in high relief on a silk ground. A Jewish symbol, such as an ark containing a Torah scroll, is sometimes embroidered in the center orphrey (Fig. 11).

In Ashkenazic communities the custom arose to adorn the Torah further by placing a shield (*tas*) in front of its textile mantle. As more than one Torah scroll was usually kept in the Torah ark, and as it was customary to read from more than one scroll on the festivals, identifying plates were placed, during the late Middle Ages, around each scroll to indicate the occasion for which the scroll was to be used (Passover, New Year, etc.). From this practical function there gradually developed the ornamental shield, the earliest extant one dating from the beginning of the seventeenth century.

Some of the most beautiful Torah shields were made in eighteenth-century Germany by Christian goldsmiths. Their shape was at first rectangular, as can still be seen in an early eighteenth-century openwork Torah shield from Frankfurt am Main (Fig. 12). Also of rectangular construction, yet different in design, is a magnificent Torah shield from the Freie Reichsstadt Nürnberg, studded with semi-precious stones and decorated with the crowned double-headed eagle of the Holy Roman Empire, as well as with unicorns and lions holding bells in their mouths (Plate III).

Later on in the eighteenth century the rectangular shields received such variations as rounded tops or sides. One very ornate shield with a rounded top, from eighteenth-century Hungary, displays, in addition to the traditional motifs, biblical figures such as David, Solomon, Moses, Aaron, Abraham, and Isaac (Fig. 14). Much simpler in design is a Torah shield from nineteenth-century München, depicting two powerful heraldic lions which rest below the Tablets of the Law and a plate inscribed with the word *Pesach* (Passover) (Fig. 13).

Quite different in design from traditional shields is a simple but elegant Torah shield made in modern Israel by David Gumbel. Oval in shape, it has the burning bush as its main decorative motif (Fig. 8).

To place even greater emphasis on the Torah's royal character, and to prevent the reader from touching the sacred text with his hand, a special pointer (*yad*) was fashioned from the sixteenth century on. At times resembling a royal scepter, these pointers, made of wood, ivory or precious metals, assumed a wide variety of shapes. Very popular in Europe were pointers which terminated in the shape of a human hand, its index finger usually extended and often adorned with semi-precious stones. Elaborate examples of pointers featuring handles adorned with lions and with crown motifs come from Galicia (Fig. 15), while much plainer pointers come from Holland, Germany, and other Jewish communities (Fig. 16).

A textile adornment of the Torah ark is the Torah curtain (*parochet*). In many Sephardic congregations, this curtain was generally placed behind the doors of the Torah ark, while in Ashkenazic congregations it was placed in front of the ark doors, where it occupied a more prominent position. Rich Ashkenazic Jews donated to their synagogues exquisitely embroidered curtains that often carried their names, their birthplaces, the names of their wives, and the dates and occasions of their gifts. Hence, it is not unusual to find large synagogues possessing many different Torah curtains, specially earmarked for specific occasions and holidays such as circumcision, marriage, High Holy Days, etc. These curtains are distinguishable either by color (as, for instance, a white curtain for the High Holy Days) or by appropriate inscriptions.

Some of the oldest curtains preserved today are from Bohemia–Moravia. These, like most Torah curtains, are the work of Jewish hands. The earliest extant, the work of Solomon and his son Pinchas Perlsticker, dates from 1592. The center of these curtains was made from a rare piece of material, often a hundred years older than the actual curtain, while the border of the curtain was filled with embroidered decoration usually containing traditional symbols and an inscription. The fabrics used represent a veritable history of textile designs from the Middle Ages on.

Splendid curtains have also been preserved from late seventeenth-century Italy sometimes with the names of their pious women embroiderers. A favorite motif, placed in the center of these curtains, is the giving of the tablets of the law at Sinai, which is sometimes surrounded by symbols pertaining to the annual holiday cycle (Figs. 17, 18).

Curtains from the Ottoman Empire of the seventeenth century sometimes follow the pattern of Moslem prayer rugs. They usually carry a quotation from Psalms 118:20: "This is the gate of the Lord, the righteous shall enter into it" (Fig. 19).

In eighteenth-century Germany, curtain textiles were ornamented and covered with a wealth of embroidery and a stereotyped pattern of decorative motifs. Usually present, aside from the inscription, were two lions or griffins holding up the crown of the Torah, and two twisted columns with vines, said to represent the columns of Solomon's Temple. A typical example of such a curtain, made by the professional embroiderer Jakob Koppel Gans in 1772, is among the survivors of the Nazi destruction (Fig. 20).

The curtain (parochet) adorning the Torah ark may have been intended as an allusion to the parochet in the wilderness Tent–Sanctuary and the Temple (Exod. 26:31–33, II Chron. 3:14). This allusion to the ancient Tent/Temple was further strengthened by the custom which arose in Ashkenazic communities around the eighteenth century of adding a valance—called a kapporet—on top of the curtain. The kapporet, in a sense, also rested "on top of the ark" (aron, i.e., the synagogue ark) and, thus, usually had embroidered on it representations of the two cherubim which belonged to the ancient ark cover (Exod. 25:17–22).

In Germany, the kapporet was usually donated together with the curtain, whereas in Bohemia–Moravia it was sometimes donated separately and thus differed in design from the curtain. The kapporet usually contained five or seven scallops and carried, in addition to the above-mentioned depictions, representations of such appurtenances of the Tent/Temple as the tablets of the Ten Commandments, the menorah, the golden altar, and the table of showbread. It generally also bore three crowns, referring symbolically to the crown of learning (Torah), the crown of priesthood, and the crown of royalty (Ethics of the Fathers 4:17) (Fig. 21).

A modern synagogue valance like the one by Adolph Gottlieb, which uses traditional symbols, recalls in its sumptuous splendor not only Byzantine art, but the luxuriant description of the curtain in the ancient Tent sanctuary (Exod. 26:31) (Fig. 22).

In some Jewish communities from the sixteenth century on, it became customary to place an "eternal light" (ner tamid) in the synagogue. Usually this was hung in front of, and above, the Torah ark and curtain. This light probably alluded to the light set up "to burn continually" outside the Tent veil (Exod. 27:20–1, Lev. 24:2–3). These hanging lights of the seventeenth and eighteenth centuries generally resembled those hung in churches. It is only with such modern eternal lights as the one fashioned by Ibram Lassaw that new interpretations have been forthcoming. In one of Lassaw's characteristic cage-like creations, he has placed a piece of rose quartz, hollowed out to hold oil. The conception of this floating, shimmering eternal light calls to mind the cloud in which God revealed Himself to Ancient Israel in the desert (Exod. 33:9) (Fig. 23).

Ceremonial Art for the
Jewish Holidays

SOME OF THE MOST BEAUTIFUL CEREMONIAL OBJECTS HAVE BEEN FASHIONED FOR THE SABBATH, one of the holiest days for the Jew. As Asher Ginzberg (Achad Ha-Am), a late nineteenth-century Hebrew writer, aptly expressed it: "Far more than Israel has kept the Sabbath, it is the Sabbath that has kept Israel." The Jew from earliest times rested on the seventh day, the holy day of rest (*shabbat*), in order actively to imitate the example set for man's benefit by God, who desisted from His labors after the six days of Creation. To the pious Jew, the Sabbath has always been a foretaste of the perfect day of rest to come in messianic times.

From antiquity one of the most important duties of the Jewish woman has been to welcome "Queen Sabbath," as well as most holidays, by kindling lights. For this purpose, magnificent hanging lamps were fashioned from the Middle Ages on. While these hanging lamps, which generally employed oil, were very popular, standing Sabbath lamps, using candles, were also known, especially in Eastern Europe.

In Germany the hanging lamps were known as *Judensterne* because of their star-shaped form. One magnificent *Judenstern*, fashioned by the master craftsman Valentin Schüler in Frankfurt am Main, is a late seventeenth-century star-shaped hanging oil lamp in the form of a fountain. Between the columns of the fountain are figures holding objects associated with the Sabbath and festivals. The entire lamp is topped by a lion brandishing flags with a dedicatory inscription (Fig. 24). Masterpieces like this one were, of course, found only in the homes of wealthy Jews. Most Jews in Germany had simple brass star-shaped lamps, with heavy shafts and hooks (Fig. 25). These lamps could be lowered (by means of a saw-like attachment) and thus gave rise to the popular saying: "Lamp' herunter, Sorg' hinauf" ("Lamp down, worry up").

In Italy the Sabbath lamp consisted of a large bowl for oil, suspended from the ceiling by chains. Though usually plain and made of brass, some silver specimens are extant, which have elaborate floral ornaments and figural decorations depicting scenes from the Old Testament (Fig. 26).

The Sephardic Jewish communities in Holland and England had their own variants.

20

These were sometimes delicate silver lamps with a small bowl, knops, hooks, and a crown above (Fig. 27).

After the woman of the house has kindled the lights, it is customary for the master of the house, upon his return from the synagogue, to usher in the Sabbath, as well as most of the holidays, by the sanctification prayer (*kiddush*) over the wine, which is usually drunk from a silver cup. Very popular for this purpose were the octagonal and hexagonal silver cups fashioned in eighteenth-century Augsburg and engraved with appropriate Hebrew verses (Fig. 28). Unusually rare are gold cups, such as the seventeenth-century *kiddush* cup from Frankfurt am Main, which bears Hebrew inscriptions as well as profuse floral and animal decoration (Fig. 29).

Some contemporary *kiddush* cups, like the one fashioned by Earl Krentzin, are very handsome. Functional in design, the inscribed Hebrew blessing and the vine branch serve only to decorate, but not to obstruct, the basic beauty of the materials and shapes used (Fig. 30).

After the Kiddush is said over the wine, another blessing is recited over the two loaves of Sabbath bread (called *challah* or *berches*) on the table. While the *kiddush* prayer is being recited over the wine, the loaves of bread are kept covered with a specially embroidered cloth. Jewish tradition symbolically linked the two loaves of bread with the double portion of manna that the Israelites received on Fridays during their wanderings in the desert (Exod. 16:22). One of several explanations offered for the cover is that it symbolically serves the same function as the dew that covered and protected the manna in the desert (Exod. 16:13). The *challah* covers, sometimes richly embroidered with the words of the blessing over the loaves, were usually the work of women (Fig. 31).

Just as the *kiddush* prayer ushers in the Sabbath, so the *havdalah* (separation) ceremony bids it farewell. It marks the "separation" between the Sabbath and the weekdays—between the holy and the profane. During the *havdalah* ceremony, blessings are recited over wine, spices, and light. In Western countries these spices are usually kept in a special silver container (*besamim* box, or *hadas*), which is mentioned in literary sources for the first time in the late fifteenth century.

Jewish tradition explains that, on Friday, the eve of the Sabbath, the Jew is given an additional soul, which is taken away from him at the termination of the Sabbath. This higher soul brings peace of mind and increased spirituality. Its departure at the conclusion of the Sabbath causes the Jew to be depressed and saddened as he surrenders his heightened Sabbath spirituality to face the worries of the coming week. Thus the fragrance of the spices serves symbolically to offer comfort and encouragement at the departure of the Sabbath spirituality.

No other ceremonial object of the Jews fired the artist's imagination or engendered such a variety of forms as did the spice box. In early sixteenth-century Germany, Christian goldsmiths produced spice containers in tower form, a shape still popular today. On the balustrade of these towers, human figures were sometimes placed—musicians, soldiers, or more often individuals carrying out religious duties, such as the *Schulklopfer* (whose job it was to rouse people to worship by knocking at their doors with a hammer), the scribe with inkwell and pen, or the ritual slaughterer with knife and fowl (Fig. 32). Occasionally only one figure was depicted—for example, a Jew performing the *havdalah* ceremony, holding the cup of wine in his right hand and a braided candle for the blessing over the light in his left.

In Galicia, spice towers of intricate silver filigree work were very popular during the eighteenth century (Fig. 33). They appeared also in Northern Italy, where the sides of the two-storied towers and the base were sometimes studded with semi-precious stones and decorated with enamel plaques showing Biblical scenes, such as Jacob wrestling with the angel, and Esther and Ahasuerus (Plate IV).

Spice containers shaped like fruits, flowers, and fish were created predominantly in Eastern Europe. Sometimes they consisted simply of large flowers that contained the spices, but often they were decorated with abundant fruit and floral ornamentation, or with animals holding crowns (Fig. 34). Some of the containers made in the shape of a movable fish occasionally held within their hinged mouths the cup for the wine (Fig. 35).

A modern adaptation of the elaborate rococo art forms so popular in Eastern Europe in the eighteenth and nineteenth centuries can be seen in the spice tower fashioned by the late American craftsman Ilya Schor (Fig. 36).

Sometimes interesting forms were devised by combining the spice box with the candle holder used in the *havdalah* ceremony. In some examples, four adjustable tapering rods to hold the candle rise from a rectangular box, containing a drawer for spices, which is either set on a plain shaft or supported by a figure. In others, a socket to hold the *havdalah* candle was added on top of the cover of the silver wine goblet (Fig. 37).

Aside from the spice box, the *chanukkah* lamp is the only ceremonial object of the Jew that can boast so great a variety of forms and materials. Made of stone, clay, silver, brass, pewter, copper, porcelain, and glass, specimens of the *chanukkah* lamp exist from almost every country.

The festival of *Chanukkah* (dedication) recalls the historic Hasmonean victory over the Syrians and the rededication of the Temple in Jerusalem in 165 B.C. Rabbinic tradition records that on that occasion the oil in the Temple was sufficient for only one day, but miraculously burned for eight. In commemoration of this miracle, the *chanukkah* lights are kindled, one on the first night and one more on each subsequent night than on the preceding night, during the eight-day celebration. A ninth servant light (*shammash*), usually placed higher than the other lights, is used to kindle the remaining eight. Its original function, however, was to render the other lights usable, since the *chanukkah* lights themselves could not be used for secular purposes.

Simple Roman and Byzantine clay oil lamps probably served as the earliest *chanukkah* lamps. In the later Middle Ages, the most common type of *chanukkah* lamp developed, a form which, with variations, has maintained itself for centuries. This was a bench-type oil lamp having a triangular back with a trefoil at its apex. The earliest surviving examples of this type, said to be from the fourteenth century because of their use of Gothic motifs, were at first hung on the left doorpost of the house. In different countries variations in the backpiece soon began to appear, not only in form but in decoration also. A drip pan was added under the oil burners, and sides were added to the backpiece to allow the lamp to be placed on a table or window sill.

In seventeenth- and eighteenth-century Italy, the lamps were usually made of bronze and employed late Renaissance ornamentation, such as dolphins, centaurs, putti, and cornucopia. The ornamentation was occasionally surmounted by a representation of Judith since, in medieval Jewish folklore, she had become associated with the chanukkah holiday (Fig. 38).

In eighteenth-century Holland, simple brass lamps with floral and heart decorations were more common. Magnificent silver lamps were also produced, which, in Holland, carried floral ornamentation (Fig. 39) and, in England, scenes from the lives of the prophets Elijah and Elisha (Fig. 40).

Eastern Europe preferred silver filigree and bronze lamps of the candle-burning variety, replete with animal and bird forms. These sometimes had two servant lights, which were attached not only for symmetry but for use on the Sabbath as well.

Large silver lamps utilizing architectural forms began to appear in Eastern Europe and in Germany during the eighteenth century. One unusual German specimen from 1814 is in the form of a classical building with columns and a pediment. The eight oil phials are in the shape of lions (Fig. 41).

Along with the development of the bench-type chanukkah lamp, there arose in the Middle Ages the custom of placing a large standing lamp in the synagogue to the right of the Torah ark. This lamp was kindled on Chanukkah for the sake of wayfarers and others who could not kindle the lights at home. These large lamps, in shape often resembling the seven-branched Temple menorah, had, of course, two additional light arms. This type of lamp, in smaller format, also found its way into the Jewish home. In seventeenth- and eighteenth-century Frankfurt am Main, master craftsmen fashioned magnificent silver lamps of this variety, their arms decorated with blossoms and bell forms, the center shaft topped by Judith holding the head of Holofernes (Plate V). From eighteenth-century Poland comes a rare lamp of this type, fashioned in the shape of an oak tree. A bear is seen climbing up the trunk of the tree to reach a honey pot, while below a hunter aims his gun at the bear (Fig. 42).

During the nineteenth century, Reform congregations, without reference to Chanukkah, introduced into their so-called temples the basic form of the ancient menorah, with its seven branches, which had stood in the Temple at Jerusalem. An interesting departure from the now conventional type of seven-branched menorah is a contemporary one by the American sculptor Seymour Lipton. Its wavelike folded metal sections suggest plant forms; its seven irregular round cups, designed to hold candles, resemble tender protective buds (Fig. 43).

Other holidays, too, afforded opportunities for the fashioning of ceremonial objects. During the High Holyday season, celebrated in the late summer or early fall, an ancient wind instrument, known in Hebrew as the shofar, is sounded. Usually made of a ram's horn, the shofar plays an especially important role in the Rosh Hashanah (New Year) services of the synagogue. Its purpose, according to tradition, is to awaken the slumbering conscience of every Jew to prayer and repentance during this solemn season of judgment. In keeping with Jewish legal proscription, the shofar is generally plain, although there are some that have a simple decoration or a biblical text etched on their surfaces.

The traditional Yom Kippur (Day of Atonement) dress of the male worshiper is a loose white linen garment, called a kittel or sargenes, the selfsame garment in which every orthodox male Jew is to be buried. Although the kittel was often tied, or girdled, with a rope (symbolically to divide the "baser" from the "purer" parts of the body), it has become customary since the eighteenth century, especially in Eastern Europe, to substitute a belt secured by means of a silver buckle. The penitent worshiper is traditionally likened on that day to the ministering angels whose sinless record is as white as snow, and the cartouche on the belt buckle, which is sometimes flanked by two lions, carries the Day of Atonement prayer which emphasizes this idea: "For on this day shall atonement be made for you to cleanse you of all your sins; you shall be clean before the Lord" (Lev. 16:30) (Fig. 44).

During *Sukkot,* the Feast of Booths, the Jew builds a *sukkah* (booth), in which he partakes of his meals and recites his prayers for the seven-day period of the holiday. The roof of the *sukkah* is covered with branches in such a way that sunlight penetrates it by day and the stars can be seen through it at night, while inside it is adorned with fruits, vegetables, and flowers. In the eighteenth and nineteenth centuries, the wooden walls of some *sukkot* were painted with traditional symbols, biblical scenes, and naïve views of Jerusalem. The *sukkah* itself symbolically reminds the Jew of the divine protection afforded his ancestors when they dwelt in booths during their desert wanderings (Lev. 23:42). Its decoration with fruits and vegetables emphasizes the fact that *Sukkot* is also a festival of thanksgiving for the abundance of the harvest (Deut. 16:13–15).

The agricultural aspect of this festival (Lev. 23:40) is further emphasized at synagogue services by the use of four agricultural specimens—the *lulav* (a branch of a palm tree), to which are bound three myrtle twigs and two willow branches, and the *etrog* (citron). It became customary to place the *etrog,* when not in use, in a special container to protect it, since any damage would make it unfit for ceremonial use. These containers, the earliest dating from the seventeenth century, were sometimes beautifully fashioned of silver, in the shape of the fruit itself (Fig. 45).

During the feast of *Purim*—a holiday that commemorates the deliverance of the Jews from destruction in the ancient Persian Empire through the valiant heroism of Mordecai and his cousin Esther—the *Megillat Ester* (Scroll of Esther) is read in the synagogue. Often written on parchment or leather, the Scroll of Esther differs from the Torah scroll in that it has only one stave instead of two. While those Esther scrolls that are read in the synagogue are undecorated, many of the ones made for private use since the sixteenth century are richly adorned with ornamentation or with scenes of the Esther story. Frequently a cylindrical case of precious metal, wood, or ivory, fashioned to hold the Esther scroll, repeats the ornamentation of the scroll, or is itself decorated with scenes from the Esther story (Fig. 46).

During the reading of the Scroll of Esther in the synagogue, the children of the congregation hold special noisemakers called *Purim Grogger,* which they rattle each time the name of the accursed Haman is mentioned. The rattles, obviously introduced to sustain the children's interest in the reading and to keep them amused, were usually made of wood, although occasionally silver ones were produced. These silver rattles sometimes have floral decoration or a depiction of Haman on the gallows, as well as the words: "Cursed be Haman."

The joyous occasion of *Purim* is also traditionally marked by the exchange of gifts with friends and the giving of aid to the poor. For this latter purpose special gift plates were designed, most of them made of pewter, although some examples of faïence work also exist. Usually the work of folk artists, seventeenth- and eighteenth-century pewter plates generally were engraved with fish motifs, since the fish is the zodiacal sign of the Hebrew month *Adar,* during which *Purim* falls. In addition to the fish motifs, the pewter plates sometimes contain naive folk engravings of such favorite scenes from the story of Esther as the triumphant Mordecai riding on the king's horse, while around the border of the plate are often the words: "sending choice portions to one another and gifts to the poor" (Esther 9:22).

On the first two nights of the festival of *Pesach* (Passover), which commemorates the escape of the Israelites from Egyptian bondage, a *seder* (literally: order) is conducted in the Jewish home. For this occasion the table is festively arranged in a prescribed manner, and the story of the Israelites' achievement of physical and spiritual liberty is recounted from a special book known as an *haggadah*. The *haggadah* has been illuminated since the early Middle Ages. Its illustrations, text, and songs, as well as the actual ceremonies performed during the *seder,* are intended to amuse the children and to impress upon them the importance of the occasion. The main ceremonial objects used during the *seder* are *seder* plates and vessels in which symbolic foods are placed. Many varieties of *seder* plates have come down to us, among them majolica ones from Italy (reputedly from the sixteenth–seventeenth centuries, although this early dating has been questioned), which contain biblical and festival scenes in oval cartouches around the borders.

The most common form used for the *seder* plate was the circular flat type, generally made of pewter, which in the seventeenth century usually had a broad rim and in the eighteenth century a narrow rim with a reeded or waved edge. The pewter *seder* plates, like the plates for gifts on *Purim,* differed from ordinary tableware only in the Hebrew inscriptions and the varied designs engraved on them. One such *seder* plate, typical of the kind, was engraved by a Jewish folk artist, Joel ben Jehudah, in Germany in 1779. In its center is a five-pointed star with the Passover lamb; around its rim are scenes illustrating the song "An Only Kid," which is sung at the conclusion of the *seder* service (Fig. 47).

Since the three cakes of *mazzot* (unleavened bread) used during the *seder* service are supposed to be separated from each other, the custom arose in the eighteenth century of fashioning three-tiered *seder* containers. Aside from the three compartments for the *mazzot,* these containers, which were occasionally made of silver, had vessels to hold the symbolic foods. An unusual *seder* container of this type, made in 1815 in Vienna, has six statuettes holding on their heads, or in their hands, vessels for the prescribed symbolic foods (Fig. 48). Prominently placed in the center of the top tier of the container is the figure of Moses bearing on his head a stand for the cup of Elijah. This is a special wine cup which came to be used in the late seventeenth century, and it is set aside for the prophet Elijah, who is eagerly awaited on the *seder* night when, it is believed, he will announce the coming of the Messiah. There are silver "Elijah cups," which actually depict the Messiah riding on a donkey, preceded by the prophet Elijah blowing the *shofar* (ram's horn) (Fig. 49).

The *seder* afforded the pious womenfolk many opportunities to display their skills by embroidering covers for the *mazzot,* towels for the prescribed hand-washings, and covers for the cushion on which the head of the household reclined throughout the *seder* service. While the Hebrew inscriptions, depictions of biblical episodes, *seder* scenes, and animal and floral decorations commonly reveal, in their colorful and naive conception, the work of unskilled hands, they do testify to a genuine folk art. A typical *seder* hand towel embroidered in Germany in 1821 has, in addition to floral and animal decoration, a scene of a man leading a lamb by a rope, probably an allusion to the sacrificial Passover lamb and to the song "An Only Kid" (Fig. 50).

Every evening, beginning on the second night of Passover, the observant Jew counts the days of a seven-week period that culminates in the festival of *Shavuot* (Pentecost, Lev. 23:15–16). The *omer* (i.e., the first sheaf of the harvest), which in ancient times was offered at the Temple in Jerusalem on the second day of Passover, has given the counting its name (*sefirat ha-omer*). To simplify the counting, *omer* calendars were fashioned—at times simple unadorned tablets or books, at other times cases with adjustable rolls inside. One such case was made during the 1800's by Maurice Mayer, goldsmith to Emperor Napoleon III. The edges of this case are elaborately decorated, while the adjustable painted scroll inside has three divisions to indicate the number of days, as well as the number of weeks and days, that have elapsed since the counting began. The case is topped by the Tablets of the Law, alluding to the climax of the counting on *Shavuot,* the holiday, which according to rabbinic tradition, is associated with the giving of the Law at Mount Sinai (Plate VI).

Ceremonial Art for the Life Cycle of the Jew

CEREMONIAL OBJECTS WERE NOT RESTRICTED TO THE JEWISH HOLIDAYS, BUT WERE FASHIONED also for important events in the life cycle of every Jew.

In olden times many superstitions were held regarding the birth of a child. Especially feared was the female demon Lilith, who, it was believed, would endanger the baby and its mother. To ward off her evil influence, it became the custom to hang on the wall around the mother and child paper amulets, often gaily decorated with animals and flowers and inscribed with conjurations against Lilith. In Italy, beautifully wrought silver amulets were fashioned, which contained the magical text inside the case, and on the outside generally the word *Shaddai* (Almighty) and such symbols as the Tablets of the Law and the seven-branched lampstand (Figs. 51*a, b*).

On the eighth day following the birth of a male child, it is customary to have him circumcised in order, as the liturgy puts it, to "make him enter into the *brit* [covenant] of Abraham our father." During this ceremony, use was often made of a beautifully carved chair or bench, known as the "chair or throne of Elijah," since the prophet Elijah was traditionally considered as the guardian angel of infants. In the Italian communities, the godfather sat upon this chair while holding the infant on his lap; in other communities, this chair remained vacant. In Germany, special elaborately embroidered cushions for the circumcision chairs or benches were often made. Even the circumcision instruments themselves were embellished, the knives sometimes having on their handles a circumcision scene or a scene from the life of Abraham; depictions of the Sacrifice of Isaac were particular favorites (Fig. 52). Special oval plates from Eastern Europe, plates which may have been used to bring the child to the *mohel* (circumciser) for the circumcision ceremony, also contain scenes of the Sacrifice of Isaac, while around their rims they bear the signs of the zodiac (Plate VII). The Sacrifice of Isaac is frequently depicted on circumcision objects because, in prayers recited by the father and the circumciser, the pious hope is expressed that the act of circumcision may be accredited to them as if they brought the child to the altar of God as a sacrifice, just as Abraham did with Isaac.

Of major importance in the ceremonial art of the Jews are the many objects fashioned specifically for the Jewish wedding. In former times it was customary for the bride and groom, prior to the wedding, to exchange gifts (*sivlonot*), which were conveyed from one to the other by the rabbi or by some other dignitary of the Jewish community. These gifts, as Johann Jakob Schudt informs us in his *Jüdische Merckwürdigkeiten* of 1714, often consisted of a special silvergilt belt for the bride, and sometimes a *gantz silbernen oder mit silbernen Buckeln besetzten Gürtel* for the groom. Such marriage belts, beautiful examples of which are still extant, were very popular in seventeenth-century Frankfurt am Main (Fig. 54). Other favorite gifts were exquisitely ornamented silver bindings for liturgical books and Bibles. Especially popular in Italy, these often carried appropriate biblical scenes or the family coat of arms (Fig. 57). In Eastern Europe filigree work was often used, like that found on a silver cover, accompanied by two signs of the zodiac and a crown (Fig. 53).

Since ancient times the bride has been regally adorned on her wedding day. In many countries she wore on her head a crown, diadem, or wreath, as she still does in some Oriental Jewish communities (Fig. 55). The wedding itself took place under a *chuppah* (now usually a portable canopy). After the blessing was made over the cup of wine, the groom recited the betrothal formula and placed the ring on the index finger of the right hand of his bride. The use of wedding rings dates from the Middle Ages. Usually these were plain circlets, although extremely large and precious rings were probably used during the ceremony, especially in Northern Italy, during the sixteenth to eighteenth centuries. Said to have been the property of the congregation, these gold rings were richly adorned, often with filigree and enamel decoration. Sometimes they carried the words *mazzal tov* (good luck, literally: under an auspicious constellation) and were crowned by a house—perhaps alluding to the new home which, it was hoped, would be established with good fortune by the couple (Fig. 56).

As part of the wedding ceremony it became customary to read the *ketubbah* (marriage contract), which stipulated the legal obligations of the husband toward his wife. Some of these parchment *ketubbot* were richly adorned, especially those emanating from seventeenth- and eighteenth-century Italy. Veritable masterpieces of scribal and illuminative art, they display a variety of ornamental patterns and figural depictions, often including representations of biblical scenes alluding to the Hebrew name of the groom or bride. A beautiful marriage contract from Ancona, Italy, dated 1692, shows two angels flanking the Tablets of the Law, while Moses, shown twice, points to them with uplifted arms (Fig. 61).

Since medieval times, most Jewish communities have had an organization, now known as the *chevrah kaddisha* (Holy Society), which takes care of the sick and of details pertaining to the burial of the dead. Generally, once a year, the members of the society observed a special day on which they fasted and offered penitential prayers. This day was concluded with a banquet, for which large wine beakers were specially fashioned. Those wine beakers, made of glass, frequently carried scenes of the society carrying out its pious work, while large beakers made of silver were sometimes engraved with the names of the members of the society. One of the earliest surviving beakers of this type is a magnificently fashioned silver one, inscribed with the date 1608/9, which belonged to the Holy Society of Worms (Fig. 58).

The use of ceremonial objects in conjunction with the performance of religious duties, whether for holiday celebrations or for events in the life cycle of the Jew, whether in joy or in sorrow, had as its primary aim helping man to worship the one God. To remind him daily of this obligation, there was affixed to the righthand doorpost of every Jewish home a *mezuzah*—a parchment scroll, usually encased within a metal or wooden container, inscribed with the words of Deut. 6:4–9 and 11:13–21, including the verse: "And you shall inscribe them [these words] on the doorposts of your house and on your gates." The parchment scroll is generally rolled in such a manner that the reverse side of the parchment is outermost; this reverse side usually bears the word *Shaddai* (Almighty), which is visible through an opening in the outside container. Some ornate silver cases are extant from the eighteenth century. Many of them have a door covering the opening for the word *Shaddai*. The pious Jew, upon entering or leaving the house, would open this door, place his fingers first on the word *Shaddai* and then on his lips, thereby symbolically "kissing the *mezuzah*" and affirming his belief in the one God (Fig. 59).

Within the Jewish home, especially in Ashkenazic communities, it became customary to hang a *mizrach* (east)–tablet on the wall to indicate the direction in which the Jew is supposed to face when engaged in prayer. These tablets, the earliest extant dating from the eighteenth century, carry the word *mizrach* and sometimes such verses as Ps. 113:3, "From the rising of the sun to its setting the name of the Lord is to be praised." Wonderful expressions of folk art, *mizrach* tablets were often painted with biblical and holiday scenes. Some of the most charming *mizrach* tablets, emanating from Eastern Europe, are scissor cutouts skillfully combining interlace designs with Jewish motifs, such as the *menorah*, the crown, lions, and the like (Fig. 60).

Conclusion

THE CEREMONIAL OBJECTS BRIEFLY DISCUSSED IN THESE PAGES, FASHIONED FOR JEWS AND AT times by Jews, and emanating from different countries, reflect in the rich diversity of their styles and forms the unique involvement of the Jews in the various cultures in which they resided. Naturally, then, the objects from the Islamic countries reflect the dominant styles of those countries and the love of Islamic art for abstract ornamentation. The objects we have discussed from the European countries usually reveal, in the seventeenth century, the pompous dramatic baroque style with its symmetrical and regular elements and, in the eighteenth century, the picturesque and more delicate rococo style with its penchant for incorporating whimsical asymmetrical elements. In the late eighteenth and early nineteenth centuries, the ceremonial objects of the Jews reflect the cold and severe, yet majestic neoclassical style, while during the rest of the nineteenth century they reveal the general eclecticism of styles then so much in favor. In the twentieth century the ceremonial objects of the Jews reflect the vivid imagination and daring experimentation of individual artists interpreting traditional symbols with new forms and materials. These may be the results of the Bauhaus influence in such artists as Ludwig Wolpert, who recognizes the need for functional expression in reshaping ceremonial objects (Fig. 10), or they may be explorations in space sculpture as with Ibram Lassaw, whose works try to break through the limiting tradition of enclosed surface sculpture (Fig. 23).

While the ceremonial objects of the Jews have generally reflected in their styles the dominant contemporary styles of the countries where they originated, much of their symbolism and many of their motifs have specifically Jewish connotations. Thus putti, centaurs, garlands, and animal and floral decoration may merely reflect the popular ornamentation of the countries in which the objects were fashioned, but the depiction of a lion usually refers to the lion of Judah, three crowns to the crowns of Torah, Priesthood, and Kingdom, and the *menorah* and the Tablets of the Law to the appurtenances of the desert Tabernacle and and the Temple.

As many of the objects originating in the Middle Ages were fashioned by Christian silversmiths, it is natural that these Christian smiths adapted Christian forms for Jewish use, particularly in instances where no tradition for these objects existed. Understandably then, spice containers in tower form are, in shape, not unlike monstrance and reliquary containers, just as Torah crowns often resemble royal crowns or crowns of the Madonna. In a similar fashion, objects intended for secular use were often adapted for religious purposes.

30

Such household items as the popular Augsburg cups or the many pewter tableware plates were adapted from the secular environment and became Jewish by the addition of Hebrew inscriptions. Belts intended for carrying keys were used for symbolic marriage belts, and fish-shaped silver containers used as needleboxes became adapted as spice boxes. On the other hand, objects such as the *etrog* container, which was sometimes made in the shape of the fruit, had no Christian counterparts and constituted a distinctively Jewish form.

The ceremonial art of the Jews reveals the taste of rich Jewish patrons who commissioned objects from outstanding Christian silversmiths such as Valentin Schüler of Frankfurt am Main (Fig. 24), from skilled Jewish silversmiths of Eastern Europe, whose names are unknown to us today, and from Myer Myers of Colonial and Early National America (Figs. 5a, b). It reveals, as well, the pious dedication of unskilled humble hands which, using common peasant art motifs, embroidered textiles, engraved pewter plates, have left us exquisite examples of a Jewish folk art, dependent though it is on peasant art.

The ceremonial art of the Jews testifies finally to the diversity of Judaism, for not only did the form and decoration of the ceremonial objects vary from country to country and century to century, but the specific objects used differ widely. It reveals the flexibility and adaptability of Judaism, which introduced new objects as late as the eighteenth century—for instance, the three-tiered *seder* container and the *kapporet*—in order to meet specific needs growing out of the dominant cultural environment. Yet for all its diversity, the cere-monial art of the Jews displays an essential unity—the striving of the Jew at all times to fulfill his religious obligations to God in the "beauty of holiness."

List of Illustrations

35. Spice Container. Silver. Eastern Europe, nineteenth century. Collection of Leon J. Obermayer, Philadelphia, Pennsylvania.
36. Spice Container. Silver. New York, 1948. Artist: Ilya Schor. Collection of Charles E. Feinberg, Detroit, Michigan.
37. Kiddush Cup with Havdalah Candleholder. Silver. Bamberg, Germany, eighteenth century. The Jewish Museum, Cincinnati, Ohio.
38. Chanukkah Lamp. Brass. Italy, *ca.* seventeenth century. The Jewish Museum, Cincinnati, Ohio.
39. Chanukkah Lamp. Silver. Den Haag, Holland, early eighteenth century. Master: Hermanus van Gulik. Joods Historisch Museum, Amsterdam.
40. Chanukkah Lamp. Silver. England, 1712. Master: Richard Edwards (?). Spanish and Portuguese Synagogue, London, England.
41. Chanukkah Lamp. Silver. Germany, 1814. The Jewish Museum, Cincinnati, Ohio.
42. Chanukkah Lamp. Silver, partly gilt. Poland, eighteenth century. The Jewish Museum, Cincinnati, Ohio.
43. Menorah. Nickel, silver, and steel. New York, 1954. Artist: Seymour Lipton. Temple Israel, Tulsa, Oklahoma.
44. Belt Buckle for Day of Atonement. Silver. Eastern Europe, nineteenth century. The Jewish Museum, Cincinnati, Ohio.
45. Container for Etrog. Silver gilt. Augsburg, Germany, *ca.* 1670. The Jewish Museum, New York.
46. Case for Scroll of Esther. Silver. Eastern Europe, nineteenth century. The Jewish Museum, Cincinnati, Ohio.
47. Seder Plate. Pewter. Germany, 1779. Engraver: Joel ben Jehudah. The Jewish Museum, Cincinnati, Ohio.
48. Seder Container. Silver. Vienna, Austria, 1815. The Jewish Museum, Cincinnati, Ohio.
49. Wine Cup for Prophet Elijah. Silver. Poland, eighteenth century. The Jewish Museum, New York.
50. Seder Hand Towel. Embroidery on silk. South Germany, 1821. The Jewish Museum, Cincinnati, Ohio.
51a. Amulet. Silver, partly gilt. Italy, eighteenth century. The Jewish Museum, Cincinnati, Ohio.
51b. Amulet. Silver, partly gilt. Italy, eighteenth century. The Jewish Museum, Cincinnati, Ohio.
52. Circumcision Knife. Handle: Porcelain, gold and enamel decoration; blade is later addition. Germany, 1733. The Jewish Museum, New York.
53. Book Cover. Silver. Eastern Europe, eighteenth century. The Jewish Museum, Cincinnati, Ohio.
54. Marriage Belt. Silver. Frankfurt am Main, Germany, late seventeenth century. Master: Peter de Mont. Historisches Museum, Frankfurt am Main, Germany.
55. Bridal Crown. Velvet cloth to which are attached silver coins, corals and enameled silverplates. Morocco, nineteenth century. Bezalel National Museum, Jerusalem, Israel.
56. Marriage Rings. Gold. North Italy, sixteenth–seventeenth century. Schmuckmuseum, Pforzheim, Germany.
57. Book Cover. Silver. Italy, eighteenth century. Library of the Jewish Theological Seminary of America, New York.
58. Wine Beaker for Burial Society. Silver. Frankenthal, Germany, 1608/9. Jüdische Gemeinde, Worms, Germany (now on loan to Museum der Stadt Worms).
59. Mezuzah. Silver. Eastern Europe, *ca.* 1800. The Jewish Museum, Cincinnati, Ohio.
60. Mizrach. Paper cutout. Eastern Europe, nineteenth century. Collection of Dr. Heinrich Feuchtwanger, Jerusalem, Israel.
61. Marriage Contract. Parchment. Ancona, Italy, 1692. The Jewish Museum, Cincinnati, Ohio.

Photo Credits

Color Plates I, II, III, VI courtesy of Photo Archives, The Jewish Museum of the Hebrew Union College—Jewish Institute of Religion, Cincinnati, Ohio. David Eisenberg, Photographer.

Color Plates IV, V, VII courtesy of Ner Tamid Verlag, Frankfurt am Main, Germany.

Figs. 1, 5a, b, 6, 9, 13, 25, 31, 37, 38, 41, 42, 44, 46, 47, 48, 50, 51a, b, 53, 57, 59, 61 courtesy of Photo Archives, The Jewish Museum of the Hebrew Union College—Jewish Institute of Religion, Cincinnati, Ohio.

Figs. 7, 14, 17, 18, 20, 21, 24, 26, 29, 34, 45, 49, 52 courtesy of The Jewish Museum of the Jewish Theological Seminary of America, New York. Frank J. Darmstaedter, Photographer.

Figs. 3, 12, 15, 16, 28, 32, 33, 39, 54, 55, 56, 58 courtesy of Ner Tamid Verlag, Frankfurt am Main, Germany.

Figs. 4, 27 courtesy of the Jewish Museum, London, England.

Figs. 8, 10 courtesy of Bezalel National Museum, Jerusalem, Israel. Alfred Bernheim, Photographer.

Figs. 11, 40 courtesy of Mahamad, Spanish and Portuguese Synagogue, London, England.

Fig. 2 courtesy of Mr. Michael M. Zagayski.

Fig. 19 courtesy of The Textile Museum, Washington, D. C.

Fig. 22 courtesy of Edward Fields, Inc.

Fig. 23 courtesy of Mr. Ibram Lassaw.

Fig. 30 courtesy of Mr. Earl Krentzin.

Fig. 35 courtesy of Mr. Leon J. Obermayer.

Fig. 36 courtesy of Mr. Charles E. Feinberg.

Fig. 43 courtesy of Rabbi Norbert L. Rosenthal.

Fig. 60 courtesy of Dr. Heinrich Feuchtwanger.

My warm thanks also to Dr. Richard D. Barnett, Mme. M. Chabchay, Mr. Sol Cohen, Rabbi Samuel H. Dresner, Dr. Heinrich Feuchtwanger, Mr. Percival Goodman, Dr. Stephen S. Kayser, Dr. Hans Lamm, Dr. Franz Landsberger, Mr. S. Lewin, Mrs. Sidney Quitman, Mr. Myron Schoen, Dr. Guido Schoenberger, Mr. Isaiah Shachar, and Dr. Alfred Werner, for graciously helping me to procure the necessary photographs.

Selected Bibliography

Barnett, R. D. (ed.). *Treasures of a London Temple*. London, 1951.

Cantera, F. and Millás Vallicrosa, J. M.ª *Las Inscripciones Hebraicas de España*. Madrid, 1956.

Ehrlich, E. L. *Kultsymbolik im Alten Testament und im Nachbiblischen Judentum*. Stuttgart, 1959.

Feuchtwanger, H. "Jüdische Sakralkunst in München," *Von Juden in München,* ed. H. Lamm. München, 1958, pp. 50–52.

Fischoff, E. "The Patron Synagogue," *Central Conference [of] American Rabbis Journal [CCARJ]*, No. 21 (April, 1958), 34–44.

Frauberger, H. "Über Alte Kultusgegenstände in Synagoge und Haus," *Mitteilungen der Gesellschaft zur Erforschung Jüdischer Kunstdenkmäler zu Frankfurt a. M.,* 1903. Vols. III–IV.

Freimann, A. "Gürtel jüdischer Bräute in Frankfurt a. M.," *Einzelforschungen über Kunst—und Altertumsgegenstände zu Frankfurt a. M.,* I (1908), 143–144.

Grimwade, A. G. "Anglo–Jewish Silver," *Transactions of the Jewish Historical Society of England,* XVIII (1953–55), 113–25.

Gutmann, J. "The 'Second Commandment' and the Image in Judaism," *Hebrew Union College Annual [HUCA]*, XXXII (1961), 161–74.

_____. Review of *Jewish Art,* ed. C. Roth. *CCARJ,* No. 38 (June, 1962), 70–72.

_____. "Jewish Participation in the Visual Arts of Eighteenth- and Nineteenth-Century America," *American Jewish Archives,* XV, No. 1 (1963), 21–57.

Hallo, R. *Jüdische Kunst aus Hessen und Nassau*. Berlin, 1933.

_____. *Jüdische Volkskunst in Hessen*. Kassel, 1928.

Kayser, S. S. and Schoenberger, G. *Jewish Ceremonial Art*. Philadelphia, 1959.

Kayser, S. S. "A Polish Torah Crown," *HUCA,* XXIII, Part II (1950–51), 493–501.

Kline, A. S. "Contemporary Development in American Synagogue Art," *CCARJ,* No. 15 (October, 1956), 1–20.

Kremer, M. "A Study of Crafts and Craft Guilds of the Polish Jews," *Zion,* II (1937), 294–325 (Hebrew).

_____. "Jewish Artisans and Guilds in Former Poland, 16th–18th Centuries," *YIVO Annual of Jewish Social Science,* XI (1956–7), 211–42.

Kühnel, E. and Bellinger, L. *Cairene Rugs and Others Technically Related*. Washington, D. C., 1957.

Landsberger, F. *A History of Jewish Art*. Cincinnati, 1946.

_____. "Old Time Torah Curtains," *HUCA,* XIX (1946), 353–87.

_____. "The Origin of European Torah Decorations," *HUCA,* XXIV (1952–3), 133–50.

_____. "Old Hanukkah Lamps," *HUCA,* XXV (1954), 347–67.

————. "Illuminated Marriage Contracts," *HUCA,* XXVI (1955), 503–42.

————. "The Origin of the Ritual Implements for the Sabbath," *HUCA,* XXVII (1956), 387–415.

————. "A German Torah Ornamentation," *HUCA,* XXIX (1958), 315–30.

————. "The Origin of the Decorated Mezuzah," *HUCA,* XXXI (1960), 149–66.

Mayer, A. L. "Jewish Art in the Moslem World," *Jewish Art,* ed. C. Roth. New York, 1961, pp. 351–75.

Moses, E. "Jüdische Kult–und Kunstdenkmäler in den Rheinlanden," *Aus der Geschichte der Juden im Rheinland.* Düsseldorf, 1931, pp. 99–200.

Narkiss, M. *The Hanukkah Lamp.* Jerusalem, 1939 (Hebrew with English Summary).

————. "The Origin of the Spice Box known as the 'Hadass'," *Eretz–Israel,* VI (1960), 189–98 (Hebrew).

————. "An Italian Niello Casket of the Fifteenth Century," *Journal of the Warburg and Courtauld Institutes,* XXI, Nos. 3–4 (1958), 288–95.

Notizblatt der Gesellschaft zur Erforschung jüdischer Kunstdenkmäler zu Frankfurt a. M., Nrs. 1–34, 1902–1937 (Contains many important articles on ceremonial art).

Rosenbaum, J. W. *Myer Myers, Goldsmith.* Philadelphia, 1954.

Roth, C. "Ritual Art," *Jewish Art,* ed. C. Roth. New York. 1961, pp. 309–50.

Schauss, H. *The Lifetime of a Jew throughout the Ages of Jewish History.* Cincinnati, 1950.

Schoenberger, G. "A Silver Sabbath Lamp from Frankfort-on-the-Main," *Essays in Honor of Georg Swarzenski.* Chicago and Berlin, 1951, pp. 189–97.

—————. "The Ritual Silver made by Myer Myers," *Publication of the American Jewish Historical Society,* XLIII, No. 1 (1953), 1–9.

————. "Pewter Objects in Jewish Ritual Art," *The Pewter Collectors' Club of America,* III, No. 1 (1952), 3–11.

SYNAGOGA, Jüdische Altertümer, Handschriften und Kultgeräte. Catalog of exhibition held at Historisches Museum, Frankfurt am Main, 17. Mai–16. Juli, 1961. Frankfurt a. M., 1961. (See also catalog of this exhibition held in Städtische Kunsthalle, Recklinghausen, 3. November, 1960–15. Januar, 1961).

Volavková, H. *The Synagogue Treasures of Bohemia and Moravia.* Prague, 1949.

Wischnitzer, M. "Handwerk," *Encyclopaedia Judaica.* Berlin, 1931. Vol. VII, 947–70.

————. "Notes to a History of the Jewish Guilds," *HUCA,* XXIII, Part II (1950–51), 245–63.

————. "Origins of the Jewish Artisan Class in Bohemia and Moravia, 1500–1648," *Jewish Social Studies,* XVI (1954), 335–50.

Wischnitzer–Bernstein, R. *Symbole und Gestalten der jüdischen Kunst.* Berlin, 1935.

Plates

I. TORAH CROWN. Silver, partly gilt. Italy, eighteenth century.

II. TORAH WIMPEL. Linen with silk embroidery. Germany, 1731.

III. TORAH SHIELD. Silver, partly gilt with semi-precious stones. Nürnberg, Germany, ca. 1700.

IV. SPICE CONTAINER. Silver with semi-precious stones and enamel plaques. Italy, eighteenth century.

V. CHANUKKAH LAMP. Silver. Frankfurt am Main, Germany, early eighteenth century. Master: Johann Mathias Sandrat.

VI. OMER CALENDAR. Silver case, parchment with painted decoration.
France, nineteenth century. Master: Maurice Mayer.

VII. CIRCUMCISION PLATE. Silver. Stryj, Galicia, early nineteenth century.

1. RIMMON. Silver with semi-precious stones. Camarata, Sicily, fifteenth century.

2. RIMMONIM. Silver. Mantua, Italy, seventeenth century.

3. RIMMON. Silver, partly gilt. Frankfurt am Main, Germany, early eighteenth century. Master: Jeremias Zobel.

4. RIMMONIM. Silver. London, England, 1724. Master: Abraham de Oliveyra.

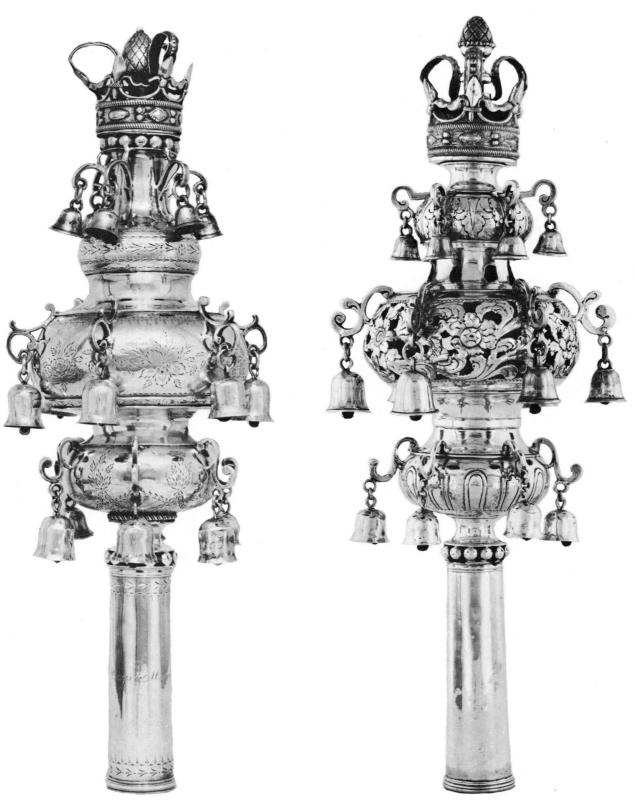

5a. RIMMON. Silver, partly gilt. New York, *ca.* 1770.
Master: Myer Myers.

5b. RIMMON. Silver, partly gilt. New York, *ca.* 1770.
Master: Myer Myers.

6. TORAH CROWN. Silver, partly gilt. South Germany, late eighteenth century.

7. TORAH CROWN. Silver, partly gilt with semi-precious stones. Poland, eighteenth century.

8. TORAH CROWN AND TORAH SHIELD. Silver. Jerusalem, Israel, 1960. Artist: David H. Gumbel.

9. TORAH CASE WITH RIMMONIM. Silver with semi-precious stones. Nablus, Palestine, 1756.

10. **TORAH CASE.** Silver and copper. Jerusalem, Israel, 1949. Artist: Ludwig Wolpert.

11. **TORAH MANTLE.** Brocade in gold thread on red silk ground. Holland (?), early eighteenth century.

12. **TORAH SHIELD.** Silver, partly gilt. Frankfurt am Main, Germany, early eighteenth century.

13. TORAH SHIELD. Silver with gold overlay, precious stones. München, Germany, 1828. Master: Georg Zeiller.

14. **TORAH SHIELD.** Silver. Nagyszeben, Hungary, *ca.* 1775. Master: Michael Gross (?).

15. TORAH POINTER. Silver, partly gilt. Galicia, *ca.* 1800.

16. TORAH POINTER. Silver. Hamburg, Germany, 1771.

17. **TORAH ARK CURTAIN.** Needlework on canvas, embroidered with silk. Italy, 1699. Made by Leah Ottolenghi.

18. TORAH ARK CURTAIN. Gold and silver appliqué and embroidery on violet silk. Italy, 1681. Made by Simcha Levi Meshullam.

19. **TORAH ARK CURTAIN** (?). Wool, pile rug. Cairo, Egypt, seventeenth century.

20. **TORAH ARK CURTAIN.** Venetian red and green velvet with appliqué embroidery and brocade. Southern Germany, 1772. Made by Jakob Koppel Gans.

21. TORAH ARK VALANCE. Venetian red and green velvet with appliqué embroidery and brocade. Southern Germany, 1772. Made by Jakob Koppel Gans.

22. TORAH ARK VALANCE. Wool with gold and silver thread. New York, 1953. Designed by Adolph Gottlieb, executed by Edward Fields, Inc.

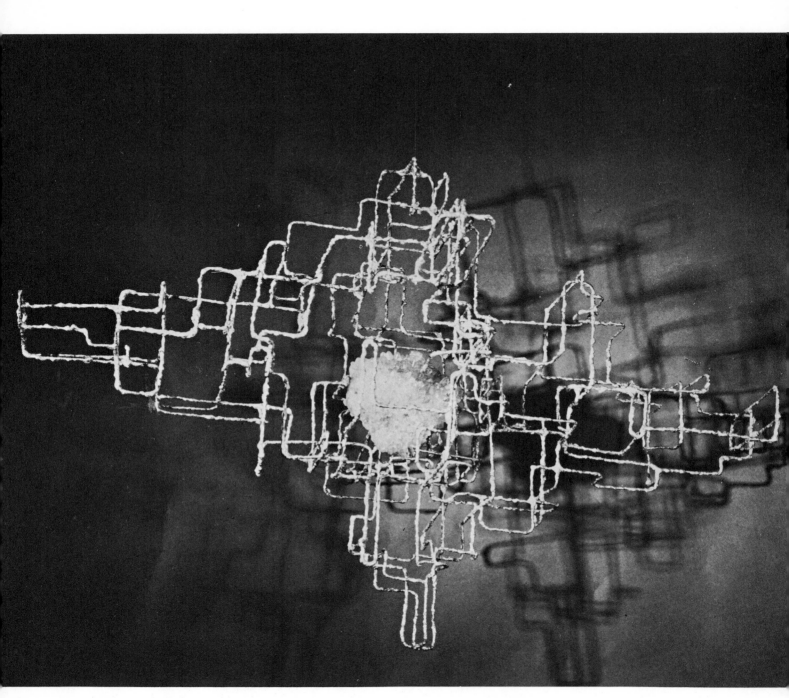

23. ETERNAL LIGHT. Welded bronze with rose quartz crystal in center. New York, 1953. Artist: Ibram Lassaw.

24. SABBATH AND FESTIVAL LAMP. Silver. Frankfurt am Main, Germany, *ca.* 1680. Master: Valentin Schüler (?).

25. SABBATH LAMP. Brass. Germany, eighteenth century.

26. SABBATH LAMP. Silver. Italy, mid-eighteenth century.

27. SABBATH LAMP. Silver. London, England, 1734. Master: Abraham de Oliveyra.

28. KIDDUSH CUP. Silver. Augsburg, Germany, 1761–63. Master: Hieronymus Mittnacht.

29. KIDDUSH CUP. Gold. Frankfurt am Main, Germany, *ca.* 1600.

30. **KIDDUSH CUP.** Silver, gold, and ebony. Madison, Wisconsin, 1957. Artist: Earl Krentzin.

ברוך... אלהינו בורא... האדמה מן הארץ... העולם

Marianna Kirschstein.

31. CHALLAH COVER FOR SABBATH. Embroidery on silk. Germany, nineteenth century.

32. SPICE CONTAINER. Silver. Hamburg, Germany, mid-eighteenth century. Master: Johann Friedrich Wiese.

33. SPICE CONTAINER. Silver. Galicia, eighteenth century.

34. SPICE CONTAINER. Silver. Berdichev, Russia, 1855.

35. SPICE CONTAINER. Silver. Eastern Europe, nineteenth century.

36. SPICE CONTAINER. Silver. New York, 1948. Artist: Ilya Schor.

37. KIDDUSH CUP WITH HAVDALAH CANDLEHOLDER. Silver. Bamberg, Germany, eighteenth century.

38. CHANUKKAH LAMP. Brass. Italy, *ca.* seventeenth century.

39. **CHANUKKAH LAMP.** Silver. Den Haag, Holland, early eighteenth century. Master: Hermanus van Gulik.

40. CHANUKKAH LAMP. Silver. England, 1712. Master: Richard Edwards (?).

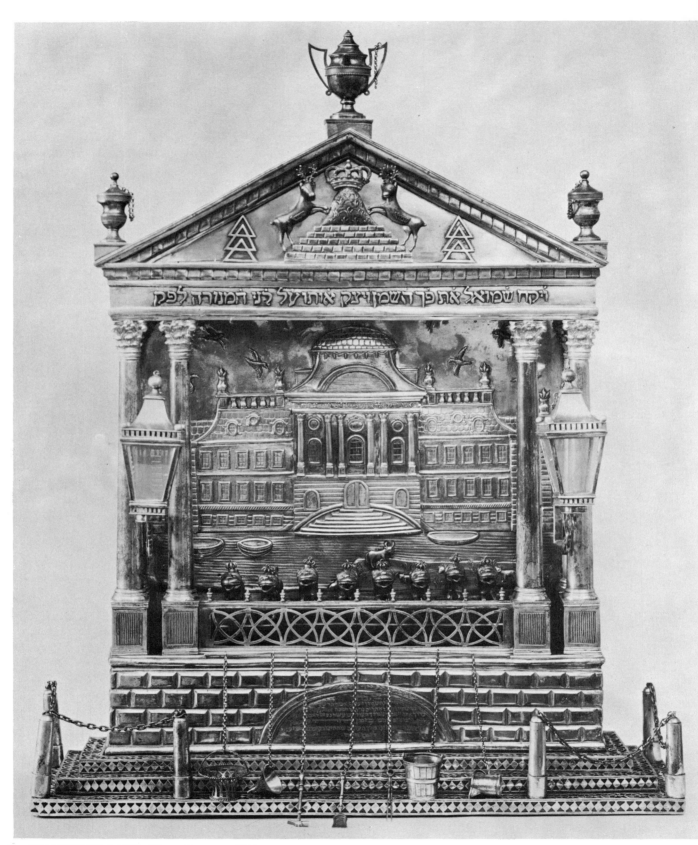

וִיקַּח שְׁמוּאֵל אֶת כַּף הַשֶׁמֶן וַיִּצֹק אוֹתוֹ עַל רֹאשׁ הַמְּנֹרָה לְפַּ"ק

41. **CHANUKKAH LAMP.** Silver. Germany, 1814.

42. CHANUKKAH LAMP. Silver, partly gilt. Poland, eighteenth century.

43. MENORAH. Nickel, silver, and steel. New York, 1954. Artist: Seymour Lipton.

44. BELT BUCKLE FOR DAY OF ATONEMENT. Silver. Eastern Europe, nineteenth century.

45. CONTAINER FOR ETROG. Silver gilt. Augsburg, Germany, *ca.* 1670.

46. CASE FOR SCROLL OF ESTHER. Silver. Eastern Europe, nineteenth century.

47. SEDER PLATE. Pewter. Germany, 1779. Engraver: Joel ben Jehudah.

48. SEDER CONTAINER. Silver. Vienna, Austria, 1815.

49. WINE CUP FOR PROPHET ELIJAH. Silver. Poland, eighteenth century.

50. SEDER HAND TOWEL. Embroidery on silk. South Germany, 1821.

51a. AMULET. Silver, partly gilt. Italy, eighteenth century.

51b. AMULET. Silver, partly gilt. Italy, eighteenth century.

52. CIRCUMCISION KNIFE. Handle: Porcelain, gold and enamel decoration; blade is later addition. Germany, 1733.

53. BOOK COVER. Silver. Eastern Europe, eighteenth century.

54. MARRIAGE BELT. Silver. Frankfurt am Main, Germany, late seventeenth century. Master: Peter de Mont.

55. BRIDAL CROWN. Velvet cloth to which are attached silver coins, corals, and enameled silverplate s. Morocco, nineteenth century.

56. MARRIAGE RINGS. Gold. Northern Italy, sixteenth–seventeenth century.

57. BOOK COVER. Silver. Italy, eighteenth century.

58. WINE BEAKER FOR BURIAL SOCIETY. Silver. Frankenthal, Germany, 1608/9.

59. MEZUZAH. Silver. Eastern Europe, *ca.* 1800.

60. MIZRACH. Paper cutout. Eastern Europe, nineteenth century.

61. MARRIAGE CONTRACT. Parchment. Ancona, Italy, 1692.